Life is not just to live,
and to live is not just to have life

But to live is to bring life
to the life that we live

THESE WORDS

A Collection of Poems

By Jon Michael Ryce

Copyright © 2018 by Jon M. Ryce

All rights reserved. This book or any portion thereof may not be reproduced or used in any manner whatsoever without the express written permission of the publisher except for the use of brief quotations in a book review and certain other noncommercial uses permitted by copyright law. For permission requests, write to the publisher, addressed "Attention: Permissions Coordinator," at the email address below.

Printed in the United States of America

Juan Arroz Publishing, 2018

ISBN 978-0-692-167038

Ordering Information:

Amazon.com

Orders by U.S. trade bookstores and wholesalers.

Please contact Juan Arroz Publishing: thesewordspoems@gmail.com

Free: **Supa Dave**

Graphic Design: **Dwayne "Man" Patterson**

Editing: **Dr. Anna Holloway, www.arh-pursuit.com**

Everything else: **God**

In dedication to my loved ones who supported me throughout this process. You made me believe that this was possible even when I did not myself. Thank you for listening and providing honest feedback. To my family back at home and everywhere else thank you for your support. For you my heart has no bottom and your love does not go unnoticed. I pray that every soul that opens this book with an open heart and open mind is blessed by what is found. To my Mother, Father and my Sister who have nourished me with encouragement and love, this is dedicated to you. Originally, I wanted to put every name that ever touched my soul in this book, but I realize that I would need another book to accomplish that. I consider you all a blessing to my growth. So, when I say thank you God, I am thanking the one in which all blessings flow. So please accept that as my sincerest love and thanks. Lastly, if you see any grammatical errors put a red mark on it and show me when you see me so I know it's real. We all can't be all things.

The Sexiness of the World

This book is for those who are intrigued by the sexiness of the world. I feel as if I have a very intimate relationship with the world. A relationship in which I can easily look at it unbiasedly and appreciate everything it offers me. I think mostly because I believe everything has a purpose whether it is good or bad. I say sexy in the informal definition meaning exciting or arousing and not in the sexual sense.

Sexy is easier than beautiful. When people say that "The world is beautiful", chances are they are speaking of that present moment. Beauty is so temporary, and it has a standard. Sexy has no standard. It's just this intimate word we place on people, places, and things that give us a rise of emotion or feeling that supersedes how something looks but how it makes you feel. Because of that I find it easier to accept this world as sexy rather than beautiful. Because, honestly this world can be ugly, which also is a temporary term. Beauty and Ugly both fade while sexiness stays no matter the state of the person, place, or thing. I know it sounds crazy and even feels like this has nothing to do with this book or what you are going through. Life is not easy, and I was told that only the tough survive but as I grow older I don't necessarily agree. I think the survivors are those who still find something in this world that excites them that arouses them to wake up and try again. Somewhere there is some thing, some place, and/or some one that makes it hard for them to give up on this world. If you are that person, then maybe you understand what I mean by the sexiness of this world. You are so attracted to the thought that maybe, just maybe, this world could be yours. No matter what you have lost or gained, destroyed or built in this world. That thought alone makes the world sexy. Don't fall in love with it though, because we all got to leave it at some point. I guess that makes it even sexier. The fact that we can't be here forever and knowing that there is so much more to create and to discover. Something to think about I suppose. What will be your contribution to the sexiness of this world? Well, I'm hoping These Words will be mine.

Keep making love and destroying hate

Enjoy!

Table of Contents

These Words
Life Station
Scientific Method for Philosophers
You
Addiction
Change
You Came In
I Can't Do This Shit No Mo'
That Girl
I've Come to Find
Slave to Your Education
Careful Lovers
Nobody Told Me
Freedom?
Valentine's Day Card
December 16th

Ends With Me
Did You Wake Up with Me on Your Mind?
Wonder
Lord Forgive Us
Father's Day Salute
The Origin of the Word Nigga
The Configuration of Love
When I Fall in Love
Size 6
By the River
Sweet
Selfish State
Searching for My Everything: A Letter to Love
Last of the First

These Words

There are Graveyards full of men who God had plans for, but did not know it
feelings concealed because they'd never show it
the most beneficial trait of any artist
is the ability to reveal what most people try to hold in
the satisfaction of a thought complete is golden
knowing
that what you have given
can never be stolen
only borrowed by the sorrows of hearts
that could never explain
the feeling they were dealing with
the emotion being spoken
by a slow pen
being opened

For the first time
it all makes sense

Hard to describe the vibe inside
when These Words that were written began hitting
every note in accord
word after word
line after line
time after time you have seen the same thing over and over
but the way that These Words were put into place to shape the sentence
that made you reminiscent

of when you felt or you thought
when you heard or you saw
when you touched or were touched
the same way
ironically, on the same date that you felt there was nothing else to discover
You found These Words
so as These Words board your train of thought please seat them comfortably
treat them as yours
use them carefully
because though sticks and stones may break your bones
These Words can break your heart and heal it too
and if you feel that this is true
well then, I can honestly say I hope and I pray
That These Words
are for you. . .

Life Station

I went to the **life station** today
filled my heart with hope, the price of it was high but it felt so good when inside
I tried fear, but it left me stranded on the way and afraid to ask for help
I began running and running until I eventually ran out of breath

Before that, I filled my heart with despair, before I went to happiness, and I found that no one was there
I tried asking for help, but no one seemed to care
I turned into a misery the people there were more than happy to share

Fed up with substitutes that corroded my heart, and tired of being left alone in the dark on life's highway

When I came to reality, and put my life in park
I tried the more expensive because its endurance was extensive

Or, so I heard.

I opened my heart tank and filled it with hope
and left for success and I'm still on the road
and it seems as if I was finally getting away and letting it all go. . . .

I saw someone at the life station after leaving despair. She said "I have some advice do you mind if I share?

"I noticed your tears and have watched you for years filling your heart with fears"

I asked why didn't she stop me, and she said, "because that wouldn't stop you," so she left it to experiences to teach me

To make me feel better she asked, "Want to know how you can keep your heart filled up forever? Restore itself and always make you feel better?

"Take me with you, I won't be much space and I promise to always keep a smile on your face"
I said that's great I'm headed to happiness again and needed company on the way

I asked her name and she said it simple and plain you got to have **FAITH**.

Scientific Method for Philosophers

Every question has an answer
and every answer provokes another question
for every problem we face, there is always a suggestion
to find a solution
with hopes that we come to a conclusion

A hypothesis proven true through experimentation
ideas are what built this great nation
but they, like theories, are meant to be challenged
by great minds who imagine realities surpassing what has ever been fathomed.

You are the melody to my life's song

You

What does it look like, when GOD takes his time?
or when an angel comes down,

When the moon goes up,
and the sun comes down

New people are met,
and new sounds are found

Old people forgotten
from friendships turned rotten

Like food we bought because we thought
we would need it, but seldom do we eat it

When true friendships are made a destiny is seeded
and to grow, constant care is not always needed

Because it grows on fertile ground
in the heart of who ever found

That life is not just to live
and to live is not just to have life

But to live is to bring life
to the life that we live

This is not a task that one can do alone
if one does it would require him to be strong

But it's good to have someone like you
to tag along

You are the melody to my life's song
the breath to my life's lungs
and my memory when my life's gone.

Addiction

Prayer for you inflicted
with addictive tendencies
reflecting on memories

Of who you were before
hoping you could restore

But it's not that easy

As soon as the high is leaving
you found another reason
at your weakest when you're fiendin'
face to face with the demon
seeming like without it you need it

Life is too hard, you'd rather be dreaming
of a way to escape the choices you made
rather relax than to ask

All thoughts of your family gone
because your addiction's your love
you'd rather be alone

To remind ya' she will always be around ta'
pick you up when you're down

But she never stays long
the nights are cold

she got you doing things you thought you would never do before
wondering what you would be before
you were under her control

You hear her so much she sound the same
so now you looking for another to drown the pain
I guess the time is now to change. . . .

Change

Change is a strange feeling of healing
appealing to those who have not yet chose the road less traveled
the tight knot of contentment unraveled
battles of the mind intertwined with time. . . .

Peace seems far away as well as happiness
blocked by relapses
and stress on a quest
to test the strength of will to conspire
against what one desires. . . .

Substitutes are searched for, remedies unearthed for
assistance along with your resistance
changing what became your fuel for existence. . . . .

Then reality kicks in, and it gets back in
hearts pound, guard down
gravity pulls you to the hardest ground
the first is always the hardest round. . . . .

New friends, new job please!?
because change even includes your hobbies
change has stolen pleasures and robbed ease, GOD please!?

Who do you think you are?

You Came In

You came in and you changed things
changed the way I am
I didn't give you permission
you just felt the need

Who do you think you are?

I mean I damn near forgot who I was before I met you
easy to forget me
but hard to forget you
I tried to let you go didn't I?
who am I kidding I,
gave you too much of my heart to go on
I need you

Who do you think you are?

You came in
and things are changing
I'm rearranging my lifestyle to fit you
I can't think of nobody
it's you

I'm calling to see if you feel the same
and if you ain't just running game
asking friends in scenarios if I'm lame
just caught up in it
or is it authentic

I mean is it real
to feel the way I feel
should I write the check to cover the bill
just to see if I can maintain
my freedom while becoming tamed

I know who you are

The keys to the chains that locked my brain
inside a mindset that a great man shouldn't be limited to one
he should be able to come and go as he please

But to make a decision
and decide which was more capable
to stay by your side
I figured it was easy to make that compromise
but little did I know being with just one made you more of a prize
because the look in their eyes when they see your smile
makes them green with envy
feeling alone and empty
they want me because they see something worth having
even if it meant grabbing
even if it meant half
and they will settle for half until
they want more and more
til' they want you to make a decision
on who you choose to be with
tired of being a secret
they become selfish and want to be the only object of your affection
so they do whatever causes an erection

only in return to be burned because the votes had already been sent in
she won the election
so I don't envy that single man's selection
it's a waste of time
well certainly a waste of mine

So now I know who you are
you are the better side of me
the love inside of me
the reason I have become the man I could only try to be
whoever that said you weren't the one done lied to me
because when you came in. . .

*There comes a time in a man's mind that he finds
that his design don't fit that mold*

I Can't do this Shit No Mo'

I spend most of my days walking in and out those doors
trying to make a change
but you know what, I can't do this shit no mo'

I spend most of my day traveling up and down this road
trying to make you happy
but you know what, I can't do this shit no mo'

There comes a time in a man's mind where he finds
that his design don't fit that mold
and that's when he says I can't do this shit no mo'

The tears I cry are warm and slow
I realize that I've got to let go
I just can't do this shit no mo'

Is it fear of not knowing what's outside that door making it hard for
me to realize that I just can't do this shit no mo'?

I feel relieved as I leave
it grabs my sleeve and its says stay
I say no
it asks why
because I can't do this shit no mo'

*You realize that this affair must grow or be
trimmed
if caught we're condemned
and though our worries are dim
if brought into light
could lead to a fight
between what they see wrong and we feel right*

That Girl

She asks "Why are you with her?"
I mean you could have the girl of your dreams
but I find it hard to believe that it's her
If her. . .
love was as good as you say it is
and everything is fine the way it is
then why are you here and not with her

Do you miss her?
Do you get the feeling that you get with me when you kiss her?
Because if it's her
then your actions are proving to me otherwise
I mean I know the reason I'm not with other guys
because they don't have that look that I get when I look in your eyes

You are special
Am I special to you?
or am I something special to do
tell the truth you forget her
loving you is insanity you should admit her
because if you feel the same
it's all a game
your ball and chain
you begging to break free
but the crime of taking a heart
could mean a life sentence
your commitment isn't a light sentence
you leave me to stay there not the other way around
regardless of how it sounds

The truth is the truth
it always seems the hardest to take
the right decision is always the hardest to make
and being in love is becoming harder to fake
but the time that you spent is making it harder to break
that heart that you have happened to take
in my mind I am wondering what does it take to make

you realize that this affair must grow or be trimmed
if caught we're condemned
and though our worries are dim
if brought into light
could lead to a fight
between what they see wrong and we feel right

With me the heaviest things feel light
and with her the lightest things become heavy

You are not ready to leave
but can't seem to stay
stay away from my arms
stay away from my love
You are ashamed of me I'm like your drug

One more time becomes again and again
I feel its best now that we make amends to be friends
until you decide this is the end of the end
and do what you know is right from within

Life is a game and somebody has to lose
make up your mind and decide which one you chose
you'll lose either way
whether you leave or you stay
because in life sacrifice is the price you pay
to keep the life we have today
I know that's an awful lot to say

My love is like a river and for you I pray
that happiness and peace is found in this world
and always remember me as that girl
who almost showed you the way

*Communication is not key
it's understanding*

I've Come to Find

I envision love and happiness
hard to comprehend what happens if
I can't have one and not the other
I feel as if love creates happiness, and happiness creates love
it's the spiral of creation
that makes us

How can one find peace if he does not have love and happiness?
what happens is,
you try to create peace
with lust, coveting, and greediness
those ingredients
add to the pot of destruction
the taste won't be the same
bland and plain
that's not love you are tasting
that's a love flavor you're replacing
The truth is simple. What are you chasing?

I've come to find
that communication is not key
it's understanding
I could communicate with you all day
but if we don't understand each other
can we
really move forward with progress
I'm just
simply saying

I've come to find
it is a process
you don't see things how I see things
isn't it obvious
we would be better friends
But the day after we decide its best to cut ties
I've come to find
when I get home from work it's you who I want by my side
so I swallow my pride
look in your eyes as I subside
to your way of thinking
I'm sinking
slowly though
hold me close

I've come to find
you can either
be the reason she is a million pieces
or be the reason why a million pieces are
put together
there's a reason we were put together
no matter if its forever
I'm sure it's for the better

I've come to find
that love feels better in our minds
than when we are actually trying
never quite happens the way that we both expected
move too fast and we both regret it

I've come to find
that we must make up our mind
and when it is time
it should not feel like you are leaving it behind
but instead
moving forward
toward
a better life
you may miss good nights
but you will be assured of a better night
at times it seems our decisions of our hearts are always wrong and
never right

But I've come to find
that ain't nothing wrong with a better fight
because better indicates once before
and I've come to find
that trying again won't hurt no more
than never trying again

Ignorance is bliss and wisdom is pain

Slave to Your Education

Don't you go and learn to be different
be different because you learned
that education you yearn
will only earn you bondage
a slave to the knowledge

I see you went off to college
that's good
you learned a lot
and you feel good
but don't you know you still the same as that young man in the hood

Oh what you figure
they don't think you a nigger
you just the same
all that education
and you'd hope your skin color would change
strange when you educate yourself it's supposed to set you free
but ignorance is bliss
when you wise up the tide is up
you don't see things the way you use to
before you were needed, now you see they just wanted to use you
then you see it was your weak mind that made them choose you
funny now you play dumb just to feel needed
just so you belong
but you knew all along
you were way too strong to stay on that plantation

Education don't have no patience
when you realize your freedom was on vacation and can come back
anytime you decide
you got on your high horse and decided it's time to ride
but you'll be leaving your friends behind
you can give them a gun, pass a blunt, talk slang all you want
but they won't get the picture in your frame of mind
you can't change the time any more than you can change a mind
even if you change the time that just leaves you early or late
but even a stopped watch is right at least two times a day
slave to your education
now you see how them laws is legislated
and the effects of no father is so devastating
and your hunger for more freedom becomes a craving
you figure the more you know the more you grow

Grow apart from belief in faith
you don't feel hate you try to understand it
rational lover
you wanted to go where the grass don't grow
just stays the same when it gets mowed
you want control
slave to the mold
of a black man who became a slave to the knowledge he craved

Laying restless in that bed you made
you forgot your religion
questioning if you ever could be saved
church don't feel the same
but oh how the Lord knows your pain

but you so stubborn you forgot how to say his name
look everywhere else but the mirror to blame
then you finally look at your reflection
and realize who gave you that brain
and smart, dumb, deaf, and blind
stupid
ears open
eyes wide shut we all the same
filled with shame
you fall to your knees crying like a baby
and you call his name and your hands go up and you realize you no longer see chains
because you now understand that faith is the simplest thing
ignorance is bliss and wisdom is pain
you gained the world and lost what brought you in it
the truth can't change
but it'll damn sure change you
just remember to remain you
because that's the only way that
Jesus's vision came true

*I don't mean sex with rubbers
I mean I've been hurt before
but not no more
well not for sure
but I won't rush or wait too late like I've done
before*

Careful Lovers

Sweet talk is for suckers
I'm looking for celebration with Smuckers
50yr anniversary lovers
this goes out to my careful lovers

I don't mean sex with rubbers
I mean I've been hurt before
but not no more
well not for sure
but I won't rush or wait too late like I've done before
Careful lovers

I mean those
date first women
six dates in and he still don't know what neighborhood you live in
Careful lovers

Those afraid to be played by clichés
reluctant listeners to he say she say
let the movie play no fast forwards and definitely no replays
as close to new as possible no eBays
Careful lovers

I need more than words, action speaks louder than those
tell me you love me by opening doors, holding my hand, respectable,
paying attention, speaking your mind, not somebody else's
Careful lovers

The truth seeking can't just say anything and they believe,
goals they want to achieve

and don't need any tricks up their sleeve just old-fashioned self-esteem
Careful lovers

Heartbroken not bitter
one more time won't hurt
learning from mistakes
not looking for the worse
never second only first
Careful lovers

The no thank you, I'm fine
I got mine
for your number decline
if there is no future in mind
Careful Lovers

I'm talking about coffee in the living room
catching a whiff of your perfume
it's too late 12 am self-appointed curfew
kiss on the cheek goodbye
through with the bad boys hello to the good guy
Careful lovers

The nobody chasing behind
wasting his time
going out for a good time
might bite if it's a good line
Careful Lovers

The living for the moment
not afraid to own it

don't mind being alone if
it means settling
Careful Lovers
real love is awaiting you
don't be worried and don't you apologize
be patient too
you just have yet to be discovered
but in the meantime, be careful lovers!

*Peace, love and freedom don't have locations
They are found in peace, understanding, and
patience*

Nobody Told Me

I never had the proper training
my papa never named me
surely he couldn't tame me
and my mother tried but was denied

By her pride to let go of what she felt inside

Rebellious youth I am

The streets gamed me
showed me that the other side shamed me
for the destruction of our neighborhood they blamed me
that cold street changed me
made me cram these codes I should abide
if I wanted to survive
but in order to thrive

Well, nobody told me

In school they told me
that in my past they sold me
before that stole me
some managed to escape, which is great, but how do I?

Nobody told me

I heard an interesting thing from a King who said that if I had a dream I could prosper and heard from a Rasta a song of redemption somehow I found exemption

from those promises made because nobody told me
that the difference between me and them
Is
and this is such a beautiful gem
That
I am no different from any of them
And
though when I became free I would see many of them
And
I too recognized no difference in them
And
those who chose to guide me away were more like those they advised me to stay far away from

I guess nobody told them

That beyond the confines of their minds they could find keys that unlock prejudices, hate, and insecurities that limited their understanding

Understanding their thought process, I felt it best that somebody showed them
because I don't fault them because like myself nobody told them
so I preach like King and journey like X
I turn the cheek like Ghandi
seek one love like Marley
preach homecoming like Garvey not physically but spiritually
because peace, love, and freedom don't have locations
they are found in wisdom, understanding, and patience
free from judgments never from sin

so quick am I to listen and offer wisdom to those
who were never told
because nobody told me

Education obtained to make monetary gain is leaving our bank accounts drained

Freedom?

In the land of liberty
Why is it so hard to be liberated?
we have come so far but it's hard to say how far we really made it
we fought for the right
to let the little light
we have shine
but, we can't come together
because we are so preoccupied with what's mine
and that's fine
it's good to have yours
because I definitely want mine
but there comes a time when we have to unite for the common fight
of freedoms we all deserve
no political agenda
filled with empty words and promises we can't keep
and truths we can't seek
without being misguided
it's hard to say in America that you made it honestly
because honesty isn't treasured

As much as money
funny
we respect a man because of his material possessions
professions
instead of counting blessings
we stressing
because education obtained to make monetary gain
is leaving our bank accounts drained

our policies need apologies
for atrocities
committed against its citizens
twisted
equality used to be based on complexion now its determined by the dividends you bringing in
because resources abundant make them less of a necessity
to successfully measure your worth
you must consider the place of your birth
but what if you reside on a side where the politicians don't consider living but make decisions for
stop taking so much and start giving more
ask yourself what are you living for
Is it money?

Well it won't be enough to satisfy your appetite
because after every bite
the tape worm of greed
will need more than you can ever achieve
I feel like somewhere the truth is missing
seek and you shall find
and the more you search
the more it hurts
especially when you realize
that the truth does
once you find it
it'll be hard to say where the truth was
funny thing about it
and I'm sure at the beginning if I told you, you would doubt it
but the truth lies within you

so don't get too caught up on the menu
trying to make the right decision
because the wrong and right line of division
can be missed when
you allow reason to overpower discernment
I think that people need someone to determine
whether they should be free
so if it's up to me to speak the truth
and free the youth
then I find it quite fitting
to tell the devils hidden behind reform
that I'm not quitting
until I'm free
so I plan to work just as hard as they try to hide the truth from me
open your ears
open your eyes come see
there is an evolution
that requires your presence
It's
not up to our presidents or government
to make law the truth
but let the truth be the law
so I don't know how free you think you are
but you'll never know until
you cross the line
and now more than ever is the perfect time to claim what's yours
and claim what's mine
which is promised in our country's design
if you don't know your history
Read it!

Until then you'll never be free
and you are bound to repeat it

Valentine's Day Card

As I stood in line
with this card I find
I can't help but leave it
because I don't truly believe it

So I put it back

I said to myself that I don't really need it
I figure she knows how I feel there is no need to repeat it
but wouldn't it be sweet if. . .
as my mind and my heart competed
my mind was defeated
because what I have to say is deep in my heart seeded
when she reads this, she will know that I mean it

So as I began writing
I wanted it to be fun, sweet, and exciting
visions of you delighted in front of your friends as you recited
then I trashed it
the expectations were too high and
nothing could match it

but perhaps if,
I explained all the things that make me like you
how it makes my heart smile
yeah, that might do. . . .

Like, if I wrote how I love our conversations about how we want to be treated and how our past is our past and it will not be repeated

how I smile when I think about **us** skipping that movie to lay in the dark

and discuss the matters **t**hat were closest to our heart

or, how I love when we get mad a**t** each other and we have our little spats

it lets us know we are not dealing with door mats

Oh! And how I love when we go out to eat
and use the same seat
others notice and then they repeat
then everywhere we go people let us know
that together we have such a natural glow
I like walking with my hand in your back pocket
so we can't separate too far in case I want to steal a kiss
holding your hand when we cross the street
can't stop kissing whenever we meet
arguing about differences and smiling when we share beliefs
how you handle yourself when we out in the streets
your expectations are clear and whenever you are near
I feel as if a little piece of God is here
and when we're apart you lay in my heart, dance on my mind
tickle my thoughts when I'm out on the grind

I don't know where this is heading
well, somewhat I do
I just know somewhere down this line there is a line that makes you mine when you say I do
if it wasn't meant to be in this life time then I guess I'll try again the next lifetime, Ms. Badu

but until that fine day
You my baby?
You my love?
You my Boo!
Happy Valentine's Day!!!!
I hope you enjoy it as much as I enjoy you.

Yours,
Real Good Hands

Sure it's easy to say I do
seems like it's easier to say I'm done
but I am so glad that y'all did

December 16th

The union that was made today
is the very reason I was made
and saved
from the decisions my parents made

At times deprived of things I craved
gave
me a sense of unfairness
an awareness
that nothing in life is given
driven by the lessons learned
from the example displayed

This day
is forever my reason
to believe in Love
and I work my hardest to achieve this love
none have come to fruition yet
but I'm getting much closer this you can bet
because of this union my standards are high and have yet to be met

I bet
you probably had numerous reasons to quit
but none more important than the reason to stay
to promise devotion, dedication, prescriptions of medication, patience
til' you turn gray
takes a special kind of person to love that way
I'm so happy I can be a part of that union

and hope to teach my kids how to love this way

She's got to push me like you
got to teach me the truth
I got to be patient with her
and lace up my boots
I got to make sure she safe
and to make sure she's true
I got to be wise like my Dad
Mama she got to be just like you

Sure it's easy to say I do
seems like it's easier to say I'm done
but I'm so glad y'all did
I didn't think much about it when I was kid

But I recognize what an accomplishment this is
this occasion requires more than just words
and to provide you with this as appreciation seems absurd
it should be a holiday to observe
the day that My Mother and My Father gave God their word
for better, for worse
I love you and
HAPPY ANNIVERSARY

Ends With Me

I want you in more ways than one
and in more days to come
I want to prove to you
the value of having you versus losing you
give you all the reasons that I am choosing you
instead of the others
introduce you to Mother
and tell her with a smile that I love her
and when it comes to forever I can't see another
I want to be your friend, your bestie, and your brother
when you can't seem to find the words let me be your nouns,
adjectives, and verbs
when life isn't as straight as you would like it to be let me caress your
curves
when you are upset let me calm your nerves like herbs
so please
let me
police
and protect and serve
you like royalty
spoil me with smiles and laughter

I want to be your better than before and never will be after
I want to be your never ending chapter
starring role actor
your X factor
Anita Baker caught up in your rapture
be your computer love Roger Zapp you

hood love hug and dap you
when your body needs more juice to produce let me be your adapter
when you slip and fall, let me be the arms that catch ya'
let me be the steam to your dreams baby I am your benefactor

See unlike other brothers you discovered on your way to find me
I uncovered what they neglected to see, which is the diamond that now stands in front of me
and I will be damned if I let one of those other mother fuckers take you away from me
So every day I want to give you new reason to understand why your search for the man of your dreams ends with me

Did You Wake up With Me on Your Mind?

Did you wake up with me on your mind?
and when you awoke did you find
it frustrating that I wasn't lying next to you
nothing sexual, unless you know
You feel that way
which is totally fine, because these visions of mine
have me running imaginary fingertips down the line of your spine
Time
with you is so precious
I'd hate to waste mine
a love like this don't happen overnight baby,
it takes time
if your last relationship left your heart broken don't worry, take mine

This is nothing like the rest
because, I was looking for more and settling for less
but now I feel like I deserve more
than a beautiful lay
willing to play
as long as I am willing to pay
for the drinks we use to confuse our views of what we really need
and help us proceed
into meaningless relationships
me bragging about popping tags and ain't making shit
You acting like you sexy without the makeup shit
can't make a check but you can make a kid

Relationships are difficult because you always wonder why the grass
looks greener on the other side
but what you don't realize is all the bullshit that nurtures its growth
whereas being together the grass may not always be green and full
at least we know it grew without the bull
and those dirt patches are symbols of making good use of the ground
to build a foundation for one of God's most conquering creations,
love.

Love
a word too often confused as a feeling
and not an action
a picture with no caption
it's when nothing is going right with you, Love will be what's left in
you
when you are feeling your worst, love can always bring out the best in
you
I'm not concerned about what's behind you
I'm focused on what's ahead of you

Our bond was heaven sent
who knows for how long or how strong?
but for right now, let's turn the lights down and lay together
and philosophize about how we will stay together
and incorporate GOD's help when we pray together
and to those who say we won't last
let's make them hate forever

So let's enjoy our time together when we are happy because anger and
sadness are real

and when we are down let us be strong
enough to know how to carry on
but if not, carry on
with the constant reminder of what you left behind you
and a hope that love will soon again find you
so the pitfalls of love I am mindful
of the women I choose

Choosing incorrectly
can surely deflect me
from the teachings that direct me
so before I lay I pray that he protect me
and in the morning I am awakened by the thought of you
I guess, I just
feel like it's time
To say that I'm yours
and that I want you to be mine

So, before the sun peaks through your blinds
I'm hoping that when you awake
That the next thought after God
Is me on your mind

I mean that is how love is made
not sexually but conceptually
that moment when you begin to wonder

Wonder

I wonder do I cross your mind
I mean when you find time
when you are not searching for time
I would hate to be blind and think that when you have freedom that I'm
not the first person you think of
I mean that is how love is made
not sexually
but conceptually
when you first begin to wonder
it's like the light flashing in the distance
then that wait before the thunder
that hypnotic spell you're under
when you paint a picture in the sky
of the last time we were together
did you feel like forever?

Like as if where you are now is good
but you know that there is better

What's your ruler?
I mean how do you measure
whether
you found something worth exploring
investigating
or are you due to other obligations that have you negating
your responsibility
to my wonder

Is it me?
Maybe I just chased a thought
that was created out of pure imagination
caught up in fascination
I guess that's what makes me patient
as I check my phone as the ring tones
hoping it's you
Like, hey!
I missed you
not like missed you
But like it was fun
it was exciting
it was intriguing
and foolishly I figured the same
it would be a shame
to think I was more than something to do
in the mean time
I've seen time do amazing things
make reality some amazing dreams
I've seen time do some damage as well
but on the negative I won't dwell
and some truths I guess only time can tell
and until these things are revealed
I've got time to kill
this poem will forever be concealed
until my thoughts become real
I will
Wonder

Lord Forgive Us

Lord forgive us
for taking your love in vain
for using your scripture to shame
for not helping a lost child find love again
for allowing ourselves to get in the way
for not having the courage to stay or to walk away

Lord forgives us
for taking for granted that you gave your son to wash our sins away
for not turning our cheek away
for going astray
for using our own understanding to guide the way

Lord forgive us
For not showing others the way
to love, to pray, and rely on your word and obey
Lord forgive us
for everything that distracts us from you
for every lie we misinterpret as the truth
for using our faith as an excuse
for sins we have committed and the sins we will

Lord forgive us
for not forgiving each other
not listening to mother
for hating our fathers
not respecting our elders
giving in to our friends

following the trends
for being selfish
behaving helpless
as if we don't know that you can't make us whole again

Lord forgive us
for not putting you first
and our desires last
for the prayers we often confuse
as questions to ask
instead of understanding to grasp
I know nothing is too big a task
Lord forgive us

Father's Day Salute

As a leader must follow
a father must be a son first
seeing a fatherless child hurts
for them to grow
and never know
what's to come

To not have any knowledge of where they are from
confusion of a boy with an illusion of a father
to be a man they must try harder, be harder, cry harder
see Father, I've seen farther
often seem sharper than my partners
from the fatherless region
where a child's support comes in monetary form
where little boys reach to find no arm
and seek attention from a noticing eye
angry at the world
negligent of girls
no rod to spare no hand to command

As I pray before I lay I ask GOD to bless
the child that has his own
grown living on my own
I consider myself blessed with all things considered
because I appreciate the sweet for I have tasted the bitter
know that all that glitter ain't gold
humble but bold
quick to listen and slow to speak

to change my pace I must slow my feet

tuck my shirt in with the buttons and buckle aligned

thinking twice and speaking once

know what I should do and don't

what I will and what I won't

limitations are pushed, moved, pulled back but always acknowledged

every decision made with the outcome played

I am saying all this to say that I had a real model on display

I wouldn't be the man I am today

if I did not have you as a Father to show me the way

so to you I salute and want to thank you for all you have done and do!

Happy Father's Day!

The Origin of The Word Nigger

Stay woke?
try Wake up
America still ugly
but I guess it likes to wear make up

Being a Black Man doesn't make you a Nigga
and a Black Woman's beauty isn't defined by her figure
and if you really want to hide something from a nigga
put it in his face
chances are he won't recognize it anyway
because his history is limited to what anybody say

Speaking of A Nigga
do you know the origin of the word?
well I got a good idea of where

You see long ago
the Spanish saw our ancestors and termed us negro
which meant black
because of our color
and for the most part that's how foreign lands defined our color
and we too eventually identified each other
now many other names came to lay claim on this wonderful thang
but mostly we were called negroes
the other names we took with disdain
or lost when we boarded that ship and slipped on those chains

Now as we all know southerners

had a drawl
most of those white folks weren't that educated at all
that made words merge together or become shorter
for example
sort of became sorta'
when you crossed that Dixie line border
and more became Mo'
door became do'
so back to negro

See those simple-minded folks couldn't pronounce negroes
so they would say "negras"
and as time moved on the term kept passing down from hateful generation to the next
they became lazier and crazier
and the word lost the "e" and became an "I"
and then came along "Nigras"

Now as the time progressed so did the Negro
and the hate in them made them possessed
they used the word with malice
and said it from their chest
Negroes went from "Negras" to "Nigras" to "Niggers"
and at that moment
Our color lost its zest
We ran from the "n" word
like it was a curse
but little did they know that a curse could be reversed

Innovative people we are

We good at taking a bad thing and turning it around
struggling to overcome until we overcame the struggle
they gave us the pig to eat
and we gave the world chitlin's and pig feet

And not every Negro on the plantation was a slave
at least that's not how they behaved
because you know like I know
that slave ain't a trade it was at this point how you behaved
some free minded thinkers knew who they were
and never forgot about it
even though history made it seem cloudy
James Brown made us say it proudly
Say it loud! I'm Black and I'm proud

Being a Negro wasn't that bad and in fact it was the only identity we had
see the word "Nigger" was created out of ignorance
but we flipped it and used it the same
We would call each other out our names
when one of ours wasn't hip to the game
We'd say Nigger you crazy
or Nigger please,
but we too got lazy

A lot of the older generation rejected the word
because they knew how that word "Nigger" felt coming off that white man's lips

So the next generation knocked off the tip and gave the word "nigger"
a facelift
that's when My Brother became my "Nigga"

See when white folks talk different they called it vernacular
but when we did it they called it slang
now you know they haven't changed
but somehow
We still giving them game

Now the word ain't quite the same as back in the day when our ancestors were in shackles and chains
see "my nigga" was the name the next generation trained my generation to claim
so when we greet each other we say "my nigga"
and handshakes are exchanged

So much now to the point that even white folks
reject their identity and want to be the same
now ain't that funny
because as I said earlier a curse can be reversed
and I'm sure deep in the ground their ancestors are ashamed
because now that we up on things these white folks done fell for the game
and if you go anywhere else in the world it's the same
because as Paul Mooney said "everybody wants to be a "nigga," but don't nobody want to be a "nigga"

So the next time somebody calls you "nigger"
don't take it the same

because even their ancestors had trouble pronouncing our name

And when they say, "go back to Africa"
tell them we did
You just brought some of us back
because before Columbus sailed the Atlantic
We already had our roots planted

Webster got it wrong it seems
Because now "Nigger" means
Nobody **I**magined **G**od **G**ave **E**verybody **R**edemption
just make sure you let them know they are pronouncing it wrong
and for that reason alone
We will forever remain strong

When you love somebody
you can't just love what you like

The Configuration of Love

I wonder what makes blue jays blue
maybe the same thing that makes that sky so blue

I wonder what makes leaves green
maybe the same thing that makes me wonder what those things mean
and perhaps what makes human beings dream

I wonder how two people can be right next to each other
but have an ocean of distance between
maybe wonder slipped in between the seams
got in the cracks
foundation shifted
hard to get it back
I love you won't put it back

I wonder what makes a marriage last until the end of time
I'm sure there were many mountains to climb
dark alleys and backroads
caves to mine
at some point I know one of you changed your mind

grew apart
tunnel got dark
lost that spark

I wonder what makes a heart grow fond
tied together by a bond
is there a such thing as equally yoked?

A man who had his heart broke, spoke
and said nope
don't worry your mind there is no hope

Another who loves said yes without doubt
with a smile on his face
because he just found love
and he knew what Love was all about

but a man who loved and lost
said love is the highest cost
some just can't afford to pay
for love to last a long time,
it takes a special kind of person to love that way

Some see being yoked as a trap
to which they couldn't adapt

The one who loved and lost said I loved my wife for most of my life
of course I didn't do everything right
and she didn't always hold me so tight
but when you love somebody
you can't just love what you like

When you are equally yoked
you both know that the ground needs to be nourished
and some can do it alone
but when we come together
to work it out

that's what loves about
when I think about that woman
my eyes swell up
I loved her
and sometimes I yearn for her touch
she taught me the difference
between being in love and being love

and every morning that's what wakes me up

I wonder why my heart had to be broken
but maybe it was for me to see what's in it
and though I have hurt others
I found forgiveness
knowing hurting others was never my intentions

Now that I see what's inside my heart
I don't have to wonder anymore
because I understand love is not a thing you figure out
it is something to explore

Start with forgiving and loving yourself
before anyone else
then let love take care of everything else

You showed me that love was more than my ability to say it but to display it

When I fall in ♥

Sometimes I get lost in my thoughts of you
and when I return I find a smile on my face
a pleasant memory I can't replace

From the moment I found solace in your smile
I lost my pride
the radiance of your spirit captured my heart
I felt so comfortable in your eyes

I could lay in your arms
through storms
and feel no fear or cause for alarm

You soothe my soul
calm the fire of desire that burns
and the sense of need that yearns

You have shown me that my arms
can reach as far as the sky
provided me with a love
that makes it hard to wonder why

You dared to love me deeply
bravely risking being vulnerable
revealed your insecurities
yet still somehow you appear to be
perfect

You changed my perception of perfection
showed me that love was more than my ability to say it
but to display it and every day it gets better

You allowed me to be free to be me
so that I too could see my own imperfections
introduced me to a better version of myself
that I could only do with real loves help

You noticed my pain
You noticed my resistance
and pursued even harder
my love for your Love
was the barter
far from an equal exchange
but somehow easy to sustain

I lost what I thought I wanted
and gained what I needed
the difference between you
was the difference between
entitled vs. deserving
You deserve it

Because you made my hearts dream come true
I know exactly what to do with you
It'll be a nice dinner for two
surrounded by few

There will be a candle in between us two
a wonderful view
as the candle flickers
we share sweet conversations
about summer vacations

A lot of chatter
about things that don't matter
about red and blue
and which one makes you madder

Then a nice walk in a park
as the sun sets and we move into the dark
the nightlights will spark
and I'd scream oh no we're caught!

And run away and you follow
with laughter from the heart
and I stop and turn around
and watch you smile as you run into my chest

My arms collapse and grasp
around your warm joy
You felt so happy
I smile and pull you close

Finally, more than a body to hold
I fell in love with your soul

Something happened to your eyes
they became mine
just like I knew within time
that When I fall in love
it would be so divine

For you my dear I thank God!

Size 6

I figure you just want to stay on my mind
that's why you text me from time to time
while I hang in the "to" like it's nothing to do

My feelings are true
but the feeling is blue
ever since the day
I felt
I no longer belonged to you

Is it me?
is it you?
I keep confusing the two
I guess that's the reason why I'm clinging to you

A spliff might lighten the mood
but it just heightens my view
of the fact that I don't think I will ever stop loving you too

I met with somebody new
but that somebody knew
that I had to let go of you
before she could ever step inside your shoe

*Friends would speak of my courage
family would offer words to encourage
but I end calls still feeling discouraged*

By the River

I find myself by a river watching my future sitting in a boat
lump in my throat
as I watch it float
I want to say wait
but my past won't let me go

When I open my mouth to shout
a tear comes out
I realize that I have fears and doubts
I ask my heart what is this about
I sit and forget
that my dream won't wait
I contemplate on my past and my future and how they relate

Have choices I made
altered my fate?
My heart is silent
to lean on my own understanding is childish
so I kneel to pray
but forget what to say
because my body is too tired from the day
and to my dismay
It's been this way
day after day
giving myself away
left unrequited
I admit it
I must ask forgiveness

But I've learned that
forgiveness cannot be attained through words
only actions
so to God I am asking with practice
for forgiveness
and typically in asking God for something I am specific
but seldom am I when asking for forgiveness
I open my eyes to ponder that thought
how often have I wondered why my prayers don't get answered
or maybe they have
and this is the path
that God had for me
What have I done?
What have I changed?
How far have I come?

What have I to claim but my own life
I reach for my phone
who should I call
that would be able to provide
guidance
then I think
I've tried this
friends would speak of my courage
family would offer words to encourage
but I end calls still feeling discouraged
Psalm 73
envious me
I stare and compare

upset that I am not standing there
or sitting in that chair
and life is not fair
why didn't I this
and why couldn't I that

Then I lay on my back
and look to the sky
at clouds that have the audacity to offer me shade
but it's the clouds that brought this wonderful phrase
silver lining

This is what they mean I ask?
it is kind of silver in fact
I sit up as if to get closer
and study it more
God is in that cloud
this I am sure

Then it passes
and the sun ray blasts pass the cloud and down to the ground
I cover my eyes
and realize that perhaps there are clouds blocking my sun
and like the clouds it just takes time for them to pass by

Patience overcomes me
the wind becomes still
the birds fall silent
the trees stop whispering
the water from the stream is glistening

the grass becomes greener
the flowers colors are more vivid
this is my life and I should live it

I'm up now
still up down
but now
I know in the darkness of the night
that my eyes get better
and the night doesn't last forever
I'm back on my knees
and I ask God to please
forgive me for questioning your ways
and wasting my days
forgive me for not turning to you
forgive me for not listening to your voice
acting as if I didn't have a choice
forgive me for not having faith
as I prepare the next life to take my place
I pray that they recognize your love
through my life
may they make my wrongs their right
may they be forever indebted
to share your love
God bless those who have eyes to see and ears to hear
and for those who are blind
let your love be the first thing that appears
when they open their eyes
bring comfort to the cries of a child who has his own
I'm grown

and I thought I was alone
I don't need that phone
I don't need that advice
this is my life
wrong or right
it's yours Lord
I'm living for you
My only job is to live in the truth

Sweet, sweet, sweet
girl, you just so sweet to me

Sweet

Your nickname should be sweet pea
sweet as Grandma tea

Sweetest peach on the tree
oh you sweeter than sweet to me

Just as sweet as you could be
put your finger in my coffee
no sugar
no cream
that will be sweet enough for me

Oh you so sweet
just as Sweet as honey from a bee
maple syrup from the tree

Sweet, sweet, sweet
girl, you so Sweet to me
I just had to write it down
spread the word around town
just about how sweet you are to me

*If you love somebody
let them know
you don't know how your love story will end*

Selfish State

You took away favorite songs
favorite restaurants
favorite shows
usual yes becomes no

I think sleep is better
I'm at peace at least
thank God for the day
then I lay
and wonder what to expect from the next one

You took away hope
I mean I thought when you called today
you called to say
I miss you, I want to see you
wish we could be together
I'm willing to make it better
give me another chance

But you rather
spend nights in the club
play dress up
girls just want to have fun
how could I deny that
gravity has laws how could I defy that
what goes up must come down
I am just surprised that
it took you three years just to find that

Where is the papers?!
let me sign that
excuse me
but I can't help but recall the time that
You fell ill
and I rushed you to the hospital
all gas no brakes
whatever it takes

I know it wasn't the best
but it was mine
I wanted more
you offered less
I made a decision
you wouldn't listen

How did it happen?
I allowed it
not proud of it
but I made the best out of it
and now that it's over
no chauffeur
to the next one

Just one step at a time
you can't run away from love
you got to walk
every now and then you got to stop
look back and act

like you don't want to return
watch the bridge you built get burned
and pray it was a lesson learned

And they say if you love something let it go
if it comes back you will know it's yours
but of course through that course of action
Do you really know what you are asking?
Pure Magic!
I don't have it
I'm a creature of habit if it's mine I want to have it

But to rephrase that I would say that
if you love something give it time
if it's truly in God's design
it could never be rushed
it will happen naturally through time
pay attention to every delicate detail
and take good notes

Speak your truth and let it be known
and if you feel a way
let it be shown
love isn't nothing you own
it's something you feel and if it's real
it'll reveal itself through action

If you love somebody right now
tell them
you don't know how your love story will end

if you are heart broken right now
be patient because Lord knows a heart is no good when it bends
if you need somebody right now
call them
let them know that you all in
before it all ends

Because life only grants us two things
that's time and energy
use them wisely
realize we
can't stop spending it 'til the end of it

So no I am not bitter baby
Mad? maybe
sad, a little crazy
but I won't let this pain phase me
I will love even stronger next time
like I never was heart broken
like I never gave it to the wrong person
I'm going to love like I never been betrayed
like I never been lied to, cheated on
I will not fear Love
I will embrace it

Because no matter how difficult it may get
you are a part of me and my growth and I would never erase it
but I will replace it
with what I deserve

Searching for My Everything: A Letter to Love
(*written for the forward of Chiquita Parks book My Search for Everything*)

Love, I was searching in all the wrong places to find you
but I never took the time to understand you
wanted you selfishly for myself
and no one else
I confused you for a feeling within
until you left me without

I Gave you a name Love
though it didn't quite feel the same
figured he would change if I gave you his name
I called to you but you never came
how can I place blame
on someone who didn't deserve your honor
as I look back and wonder
what kind of spell Was I under
to ever think he could fill the void

and foolishly I repeated
as if I said your name enough that even he would believe it

Going out of my way day to day
just to say that you were mine
and he'll come around in due time

Got to be patient
is what I would tell myself

But the time didn't equate to satisfaction
maybe it's too much that I'm asking
so I left your name out the equation
thinking that maybe it would add up to you
but in my heart I knew that wasn't true
eventually I stopped seeing you
and replaced you with him
lost myself in his lies
only saw myself in his eyes

So much that I gave
so much that I lost
I neglected to see
that it was more to you than what My eyes could see

I confused you with him to the point that even wrong felt right
as long as I was acceptable in his sight
making an excuse for why he couldn't produce
what I was missing
ignored my intuition
all in, on a mission
impossible

Broken hearted
I started
seeking you in God

I was ashamed to see
that it wasn't him, it was me

it wasn't me, it was God
who had the key
to unlock my insecurities
told me I was perfectly imperfect
I began to see
that before I could find you in others
I had to seek you in me

And after much prayer I opened my eyes
I lost him and I found you
as I grew closer to God
it became too hard to accept anything less

I finally saw in his eyes for the first time
that what I was chasing was the thought of you Love
but instead of him I should call to you
so I gave your name to God
it wasn't hard

Just as easy as a Sunday morning
clouds break from all the storming
without warning
I felt my cold heart warming
no more defenses
because God has armed me
with the true definition
of what Love really means
I had to lose it all just to find My Everything

*I look forward to meeting every person that reads
and breathes life into these words*

Last of the First

This is the last of the first
I wrote this focused on the dirt
from which I came
my place of birth
measuring my fruits worth

I would hope but much rather pray
that those who ate from this plate
of food for thought
were blessed with nutrients
that allows you to appreciate your own
and be encouraged to share
with others

To my sisters and brothers
fathers and mothers
haters and lovers
I am forever grateful for your patience
as I take this final bow
before the next flood of inspiration
rushes into thirsty roots
to produce hopefully another harvest of words

I pray they are as bountiful as this one has been
God has his hands all over this book and you
if you don't believe in him
no worries he believes in you

I look forward to meeting every person that reads and breathes life into them
I hope they designate a place in your heart
and resonate in the dark and produce light to those who like I have dwelled in it

In life
take it light
but take it
never fake it
or hate it
if you don't have it create it
If you don't know how
Be creative

To those whose prose inspired me
and required me to take every word seriously
and live vicariously through me
truly I am thankful

To God the most high
I'm better than I deserve
and from what I was allowed to do with the mind that you
have given me
thank you
thank you for my seed
for the tree that produced it
truth is
I never would have recognized my own potential

without recognizing your power

to my shining moment to my darkest hour I will forever

thank you

Be blessed,

Juan Arroz

Don't you go and learn to be different;

Be different because you learned

www.ingramcontent.com/pod-product-compliance
Lightning Source LLC
Chambersburg PA
CBHW050915160426
43194CB00011B/2417